SPACE

BY WILLIAM ANTHONY

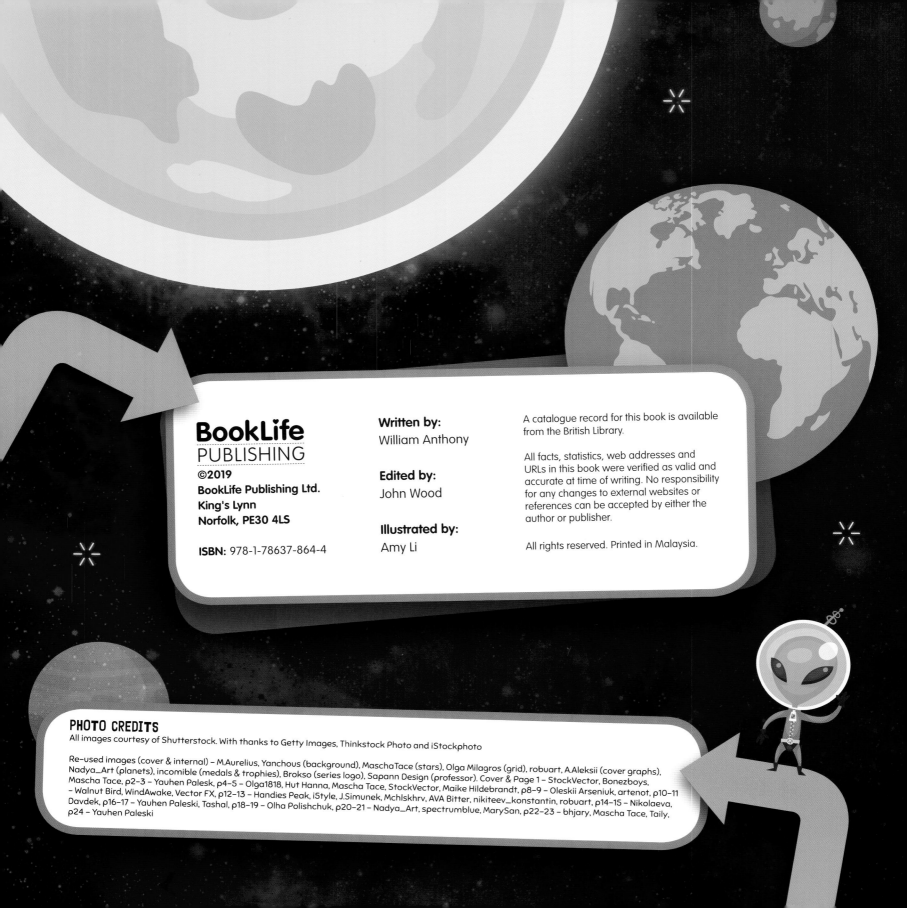

BookLife
PUBLISHING

©2019
BookLife Publishing Ltd.
King's Lynn
Norfolk, PE30 4LS

ISBN: 978-1-78637-864-4

Written by:
William Anthony

Edited by:
John Wood

Illustrated by:
Amy Li

CONTENTS

Words that look like <u>this</u> can be found in the glossary on page 24.

SUPER STATS

Numbers are all around us. They help us <u>compare</u> lots of different things to find out all sorts of information, such as which is the biggest or smallest, hottest or coldest.

FACT

Stats is short for the word statistics. Statistics are numbers that <u>represent</u> bits of information.

10

2

5

1

8

4

SPACE

Space is everything outside our world. You can see it when you look into the sky, especially at night. Our planet might seem big, but it is tiny compared to space. Space is so big that we can't see it all, even with our most powerful <u>telescopes</u>.

HOW BIG ARE WE?

It can be difficult to imagine that Earth is a very small planet. But in our <u>solar system</u> it is only the **5th-largest** planet. Jupiter is the biggest planet and Mercury is the smallest.

Mercury

Earth

YOU ARE HERE!

5th

FACT

The Sun is not a planet. It is a star like all the other stars you see at night. It looks bigger than the other stars because it is closer to Earth.

Jupiter

Jupiter is so big that you could fit each of the other seven planets in our solar system inside it all at once, with a lot of room still to spare.

1st

If you thought our planet was big, Earth would fit inside Jupiter over **1,300** times.

HOTTEST AND COLDEST PLANETS

Have you ever thought that it was too hot or cold to go outside? On Earth, the <u>temperature</u> is just right for humans. This is one of the reasons why you won't find humans on other planets in our solar system – other planets are too hot or too cold.

FACT

On some other planets, a human would freeze or burst into flames straight away.

Neptune

The <u>average</u> temperature on Earth is around **15** degrees Celsius (°C). On Venus, the temperature is over **460** degrees Celsius, making it the hottest planet in our solar system. The coldest planet is Neptune, at a freezing **-200** degrees Celsius.

AVERAGE TEMPERATURE OF THE PLANETS

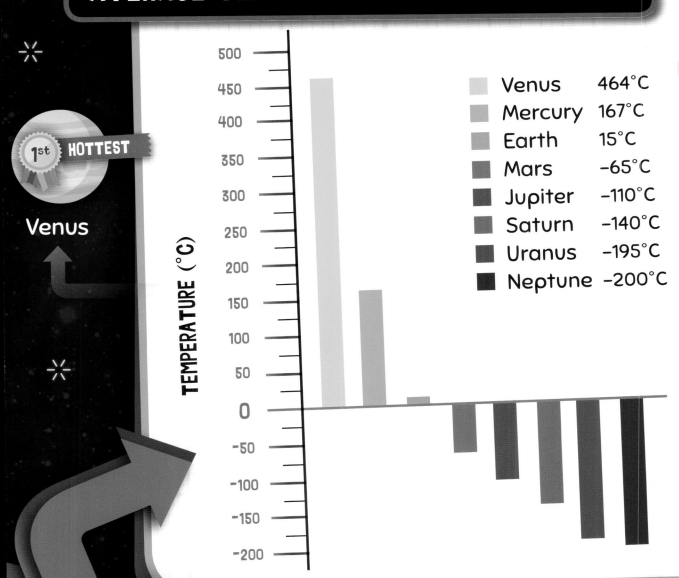

Planet	Temperature
Venus	464°C
Mercury	167°C
Earth	15°C
Mars	–65°C
Jupiter	–110°C
Saturn	–140°C
Uranus	–195°C
Neptune	–200°C

1st HOTTEST

Venus

1st COLDEST

Neptune

MOST MOONS

When we look up at the night sky, we might see the Moon. Earth only has **1** moon, but did you know that some of the other planets in our solar system have lots of moons?

Mars

STAT ATTACK!

The Moon takes around **27** days to complete a full loop around the Earth.

1st **MOST MOONS**

Jupiter

Mercury and Venus have no moons at all. Jupiter has the most moons with **79**. Some of Jupiter's moons are so big that you can see them just by using <u>binoculars</u>.

FACT

Mercury doesn't have any moons because the Sun's <u>gravity</u> would pull any moon away.

PLANET	MOONS	
Mercury / Venus		0
Earth	I	1
Mars	II	2
Jupiter 🏆	₥₥ ₥₥ ₥₥ ₥₥ ₥₥ ₥₥ ₥₥ ₥₥ ₥₥ ₥₥ ₥₥ ₥₥ ₥₥ ₥₥ ₥₥ IIII	79
Saturn	₥₥ ₥₥ ₥₥ ₥₥ ₥₥ ₥₥ ₥₥ ₥₥ ₥₥ ₥₥ III	53
Uranus	₥₥ ₥₥ ₥₥ ₥₥ ₥₥ II	27
Neptune	₥₥ ₥₥ IIII	14

OBJECTS LEFT ON THE MOON

Humans have visited Earth's moon to gather information about it. But did you know that we have left lots of strange objects there?

FAMILY PHOTO

During the Apollo 16 mission, Charles Duke left a photo of his family.

TWO GOLF BALLS

During the Apollo 14 mission, Alan Shepard played golf on the Moon.

TRIBUTES

A golden olive branch, medals and a model of an astronaut have been left to remember those who died trying to get to space.

WEE, POO AND VOMIT

There are almost 100 bags of human waste on the Moon.

BOOTS

Many everyday items have been left on the Moon to save weight for the journey home.

BIGGEST STAR

Understanding how big space is can be very difficult. We have already found out how small the Earth is compared to Jupiter, but how small is the Sun compared to the biggest star in space?

FACT

Never look directly at the Sun. It can badly damage your eyes.

FACT

Scientists still can't be sure how big some stars are, because they are so far away.

The Sun

1st

BIGGEST

The biggest-known star in space is UY Scuti. It is so big that it is called a hypergiant. It's thought that UY Scuti could fit **5 billion** Suns inside it.

FACT

Stars are bright balls of burning <u>gases</u>.

STAT ATTACK!

UY Scuti is thought to be **2.4 billion** kilometres across.

UY Scuti

15

GIGANTIC GALAXIES

A galaxy is a huge group of gases, dust and billions of stars and their solar systems. Galaxies are held together by gravity. Our solar system is in a large galaxy called the Milky Way.

STAT ATTACK!

Earth is **12,756** kilometres across. The Milky Way is about **1,000,000,000,000,000,000** kilometres across. That's **1 quintillion** kilometres, or **100,000** <u>light-years</u>!

The Milky Way

The biggest galaxy in space is called IC 1101. It is thought to be over **4 million** light-years across. Let's take a look at the size of our galaxy compared to some of the biggest galaxies in space.

THE BIGGEST GALAXIES IN SPACE

1st

	IC 1101	at least **4 million** light-years
	Hercules A	around **1.5 million** light-years
	Abell 2261-BCG	around **1 million** light-years
	NGC 6872	over **500,000** light-years
	Milky Way	around **100,000** light-years

BIGGEST CONSTELLATIONS

Have you ever been stargazing? On a clear night, we can see beautiful patterns of stars all over the sky. Some of these groups form outlines of shapes and these are called constellations.

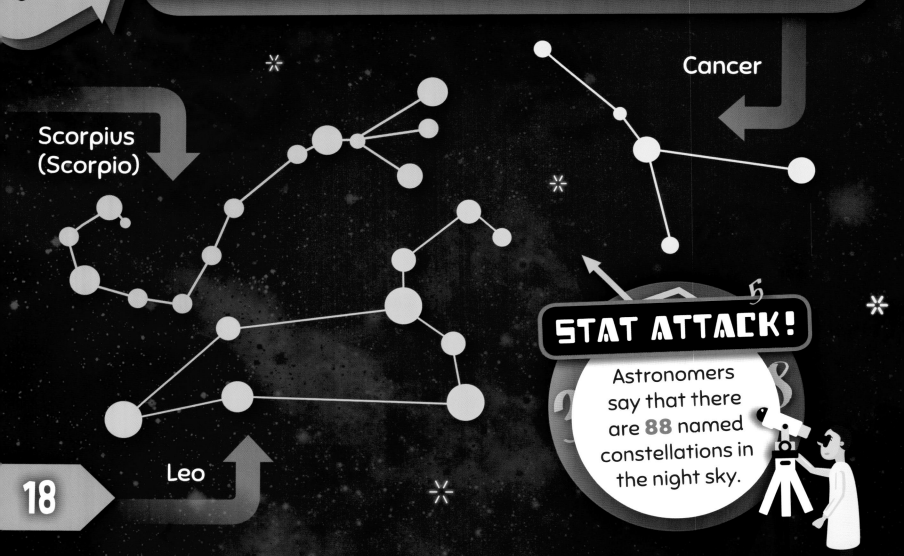

Cancer

Scorpius (Scorpio)

Leo

STAT ATTACK!

Astronomers say that there are **88** named constellations in the night sky.

The constellations all take up different amounts of the sky. The largest constellation is Hydra, which takes up **3.2** <u>percent</u> (%) of the sky. The smallest is Crux, which takes up just **0.2** percent of the sky. Here are the sizes of some of the most famous constellations.

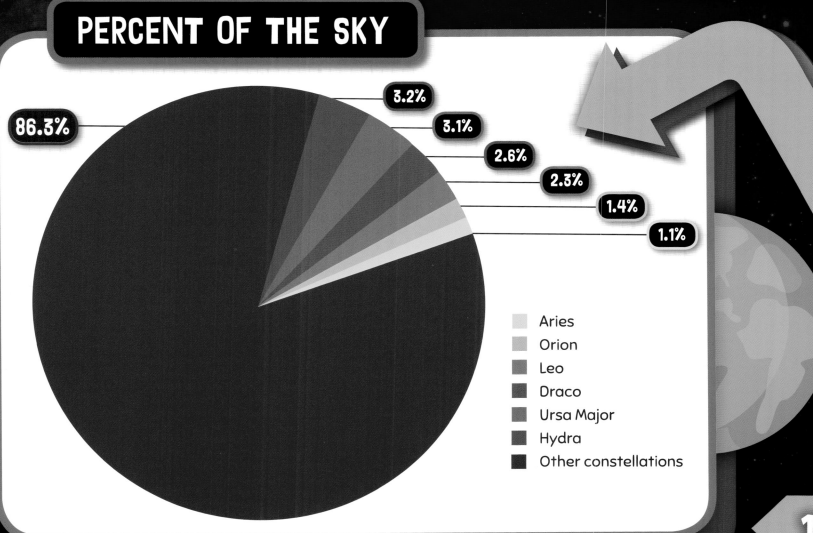

PERCENT OF THE SKY

86.3%
3.2%
3.1%
2.6%
2.3%
1.4%
1.1%

Aries
Orion
Leo
Draco
Ursa Major
Hydra
Other constellations

CRAZIEST WEATHER

Earth has tornadoes, earthquakes and big floods. Other planets in our solar system have even crazier weather.

Mercury's temperature can change from around **430** degrees Celsius in the day to around **-180** degrees Celsius at night.

On Venus, it doesn't rain water - it rains dangerous, strong <u>acid.</u>

There is a storm on Jupiter that has been going for between 150 and 400 years.

On both Neptune and Uranus, scientists think it could rain solid diamonds.

The fastest ever winds on Earth were around 400 kilometres per hour. The winds on Neptune can reach over 1,800 kilometres per hour. That's faster than the speed of sound!

FAR, FAR AWAY

To see the some of the farthest things in space, we need very powerful telescopes. We use telescopes to look up into space. This is called making space observations. One of the most famous telescopes we have is Hubble. Hubble <u>orbits</u> the Earth.

Hubble

HUBBLE STATISTICS

- Hubble has made over **1.3 million** observations.

- Hubble moves around the Earth at about **27,000** kilometres per hour.

- Hubble has travelled over **6 million** kilometres around Earth.

- Hubble has found objects over **13 billion** light-years away.

Icarus

The farthest star that has been seen was spotted by the Hubble telescope. The star is called Icarus. It is over **9 billion** light-years away from Earth.

1st FARTHEST STAR

1st FARTHEST GALAXY

The farthest galaxy ever seen has the less catchy name of GN–z11. It is **13.4 billion** light-years away from Earth and was also spotted by Hubble.

GN–z11

GLOSSARY

acid	a chemical that can break things down
average	a usual amount
binoculars	instruments that have one lens for each eye that are used to look at objects that are far away
compare	to look at two or more things to see what is similar or different about them
gases	things that are like air, which fill any space available
gravity	the invisible force that pulls everything towards very large things
light-years	units of distance equal to the distance light can travel in one year
orbits	repeatedly travels around an object in space
percent	one part in every 100
represent	to stand for something else
solar system	a system that includes a star and everything that orbits that star, such as planets and moons
telescopes	instruments that use lenses and sometimes mirrors to make distant objects appear larger
temperature	how hot or cold something is

INDEX